# My Heart Will Go On

from the Paramount and Twentieth Century Fox Motion Picture TITANIC

*intermediate harp arrangement*

Harp arrangement by Sylvia Woods

Music by James Horner
Lyric by Will Jennings

〰〰〰 indicates to play your right hand low on the strings, near the soundboard

4